GREATEST!

Love from

....

This headline's just in ...
Top news, it's the latest!
Sienna's the best –

She's really the GREATEST!

Just like a puppy,
Sienna is FUN ...

FREE HUGS
CARDIFF
LON
EDINBURG
BELFAST

Sienna is **THOUGHTFUL**,
And **HUGS** like a bear.
When you need somebody,
She'll always be there.

The FUNNIEST monkey you'll find at the zoo ...

Sienna will bring out the giggles in you!

A CURIOUS bunny,
Sienna asks more, like,
"Where did this come from?"
"What's this by the door?"

NO HUGGING
THE EXHIBITS

She's bananas for apples
And peachy for grapes ...

Sienna loves EATING
Her food in all SHAPES!

When facing her fears,
She might find things
frightful ...

Then out ROARS
a lion,
So BRAVE and
delightful.

And even when things get
A little bit hairy,
Sienna will laugh,
"This isn't so scary."

This wise little owl's
Remarkably CLEVER,
She finds her way through
Almost any endeavour.

Sienna LOVES numbers,
And adds up with ease.
"I think I've enough
To buy five roses, please."

A real human rhino,
Sienna is STRONG –

Nothing's too heavy,
Too large or too long.

She NAPS like a sloth
And can snooze anywhere.

Sienna dreams BIG
Going here, going there.

Sienna's so BUSY,
She beavers along ...
HARD-WORKING
and FOCUSED,

So what could go wrong?

(And sometimes when things
Don't quite go to plan ...
We know that Sienna's tried
All that she can.)

As SWEET as a kitten
And utterly CUTE,
Sienna is LOVING
And GENEROUS to boot.

She's travelled all over,
From farms to fairs,
To show someone special
Just how much she cares.

So, there now you have it,
Sienna is best.
So FRIENDLY and FUNNY
And BRAVE ... and the rest.

There's no one quite like her ...
It's *TOTALLY* true!
The GREATEST kid *ever*?
Sienna, that's ...

YOU!